D1716902

FAQ
TEEN LIFE™

FREQUENTLY ASKED QUESTIONS ABOUT

Social
Networking

Colleen
Ryckert Cook

ROSEN
PUBLISHING®

New York

Published in 2011 by The Rosen Publishing Group, Inc.
29 East 21st Street, New York, NY 10010

First Edition

Library of Congress Cataloging-in-Publication Data

Cook, Colleen Ryckert.
Frequently asked questions about social networking / Colleen
Ryckert Cook.
    p. cm.—(FAQ: teen life)
Includes bibliographical references and index.
ISBN 978-1-4488-1329-2 (library binding)
1. Online social networks. 2. Social networks. I. Title.
HM742.C66 2011
006.7'540835—dc22

                                                    2010021320

Manufactured in the United States of America

CPSIA Compliance Information: Batch #W11YA: For further information, contact Rosen Publishing, New York, New
York, at 1-800-237-9932

Contents

one

WHAT IS SOCIAL NETWORKING?

"Social networking" is a phrase used to describe how people interact with others online. You probably engage in social networking without even realizing it. Anytime you comment on friends' posts on MySpace or Facebook, forward a link to a YouTube video that made you LOL, share MP3s, or send an instant message, you're doing the social networking thing.

A recent study from Pew Research Center's Internet & American Life Project showed that more than nine out of ten teens surveyed regularly spent time online—and about two-thirds of them did so daily. What's more, 73 percent of teens ages twelve to seventeen used a social networking site like MySpace, Facebook, Bebo, or YouTube.

Social networking sites are like your locker at school or maybe your room at home, only digitalized. You can post pictures of friends and pets. You can shoot and show off

Shawn Fanning was a college student at Northeastern University when he created a file-sharing program that let music lovers upload and share MP3 files in 1998. Napster was one of the earliest social networking communities.

goofy videos. You can play your favorite song. You can text friends, ask for help with homework, and join clubs.

Interacting online has become so commonplace that it's easy to forget how new the concept is, relatively speaking. The earliest instant messaging programs appeared in the 1960s but were limited to networked computers. Peer-to-peer software, which lets users share files and other information, and discussion boards have been around since the late 1970s and early 1980s. Computer whizzes, corporations, and the government used these programs to access and share information. Home computers didn't become common until the mid-1990s.

It was around then that innovators like Napster founder Shawn Fanning and the instant messaging designers Arik Vardi, Yair Goldfinger, Sefi Vigiser, and Amnon Imir of Miribilis took technology one step further. They realized anyone from anywhere could upload music, pictures, or their own words, and then share with whoever wanted to see them. They could find places online, called chat rooms, to send instant messages. The age of public-generated online content, dubbed Web 2.0, had dawned.

Interacting online has its good points and its bad points. Knowing how and why you use social networking is one thing. You also need to understand how and why others use it, whether for sincere or manipulative reasons.

What's Out There?

Everywhere you click you can find a social networking site. Some are more popular than others. Facebook has edged out MySpace as the preferred social networking site. It's user-friendly, and many parents like the privacy settings. Still, MySpace remains popular with teens. The chaotic look turns off more adults, which is probably why a lot of teens still play there.

Discussion boards are networking sites where people can post comments or questions about specific, shared interests. Often, social networking sites or more popular blogs have discussion boards built into their sites. Sometimes called forums, discussion boards usually have dozens—if not hundreds—of different topics being discussed simultaneously. Some boards let any user start new topics. Other boards are moderated or allow only registered members to post.

YouTube is one of the most widely used social networking sites around. People can upload their own videos, subscribe to others' accounts, comment and rate videos, and more. Video responses let viewers link to and build upon others' uploads.

The video-based site YouTube (http://www.youtube.com) is perhaps the most successful social networking site around. Users upload and share videos. Lonelygirl15 was one of the first viral webcasts.

Webcasts are live-streaming videos used by television programmers, musicians, performers, and fans. Anyone can create a show and post it to YouTube or his or her own Web site. The children's and teens' television channel Nickelodeon even created the popular show *iCarly*, about three teens who post a regular webcast.

In 2006, Lonelygirl15 was a popular interactive webcast from a sixteen-year-old girl named Bree. She attracted thousands of fans who commented on her vlogs and MySpace page. The webcast was filled with her musings about school and home. It was all very normal until she started dabbling in the occult. Suspicions arose. It turned out Lonelygirl15 was a fictional program created by the filmmaking team Creative Artists Agency. Bree was actually nineteen-year-old actress Jessica Rose. Despite the deception, Lonelygirl15, now dubbed LG15, kept its fans and remains a popular webcast.

But social networking isn't just about videos. Some teens gather at gaming communities such as Cellufun or World of Warcraft. Some sites, like Cosmogirl.com, do in the digital world what teen celebrity or fashion magazines do on paper. Other teens seek out shared interest groups, such as Flikster or LastFM. There are communities for teens dealing with cancer, teens with special-needs siblings, teen booklovers, manga fans, and live-action role-playing (or LARP) gamers, among others. For anything you can think of, there's probably a Web-based community for it. Just Google a keyword and see what you find.

Not Your Parents' Web

Both adults and teens use social networking sites to interact with others. Often, adults use it for business. They market products or recruit others to their causes. They build connections that can further their careers or agendas.

Just as often, adults, like teens, simply want to hang out. They share photos and news with family who live out of state, reconnect with old friends, or seek out others who share their interests. For example, many children's book writers have built networking communities on LiveJournal and Twitter. Communities built around politics, art, music, family life, women's issues, men's health, and education abound.

Teens have built their own communities. In 2005, a fifteen-year-old named Catherine Cook started her own social networking company with her brothers Dave and Geoff. She came up with the idea while flipping through a high school year-book. She wanted to create opportunities for students in her high school to find and meet new people.

When MyYearbook.com launched in August 2005, two hundred students from New Jersey's Montgomery High School signed up. Within nine months, MyYearbook.com had one million members. About six million unique visitors click on the site each month. With its part gaming community, part virtual dating service, MyYearbook.com attracts teens and young adults.

Nerdfighters.com is another explosive example of a community built by and for teens. In 2006, John Green, author of award-winning teen novels *Looking for Alaska*, *An Abundance of Katherines*, and *Paper Towns*, and his brother, Hank, realized something. Because they lived on opposite sides of the continent, they communicated mostly via e-mail or instant messaging. They saw each other face-to-face about once a year during the holidays.

The brothers challenged themselves to spend a year communicating only by video. Brotherhood 2.0 started January 1, 2007. Each weekday for a year, John Green posted the brothers' vlogs on his Web site. It evolved to include challenges the brothers had to accomplish on camera. Viewers could suggest and vote on punishments for the brother who lost the challenge or

Microblogging Web site Twitter (http://www.twitter.com) allows users to share links and keep friends updated in 140 characters or less. And now, with developments in technology, users can update from anywhere via handheld device.

communicated by text or e-mail. Some memorable ones: "John Chugs a Big Mac Smoothie" and "Hank Eats as Many Peeps as He Can in Six Minutes While Discussing the Book *We Wish to Inform You That Tomorrow We Will Be Killed With Our Families.*"

Hank's serenade about actress Helen Hunt started a tradition as well. Each time his turn to create a vlog fell on a Wednesday, he had to write and perform a new song. One million YouTube viewers and counting have watched "Accio Deathly Hallows," Hank's angst-ridden, pre-release ode to the seventh Harry Potter book.

By the end of 2007, several thousand devoted teen followers, dubbed Nerdfighters in honor of a video game John found during an airport layover, had built a community. They make and share videos. They participate in secret projects that are revealed online. The Foundation to Decrease World Suck inspired political donations and microloans for impoverished business owners in third-world countries through Kiva.org. Teens join various discussions in the forum My Pants. There's even a music and merchandising site named DFTBA Music after the Nerdfighters' motto: Don't Forget to Be Awesome.

There are other teen-based communities as well. A teen cancer patient named Melissa inspired the Teens Living with Cancer community. TLC helps newly diagnosed teens as well as those who've had cancer for years. They offer "Straight Talk," a video of real teens who talk candidly about their cancer treatments, changes in friendships and home lives, and what it's like to face possible death head on. They also have chat nights and discussion boards.

Dynamic, involved communities like these are great, but at the same time many teens just want to hang out. They don't care if they belong to something bigger. They use social networking to do what teens have always done: goof off with friends, laugh, and complain about homework/parents/siblings/teachers. They just text it when they can't do it face-to-face.

And like they have done throughout the ages, today's teens use social networking to test the waters to find out who they can or want to become. They assert their independence from parents with their own little place on the Internet. They make new friends. They flirt. They act tough, then two minutes later act silly. They wonder aloud about the world and the people in it. Sometimes they seek validation by having lots of friends or by getting attention from strangers of the opposite sex. They use the interactive nature of modern computer society to try out different personalities.

Social networking should be fun and carefree, but you must also be smart and safe. In the next chapters, you'll learn more about teen-targeted marketing, online bullies and predators, and risky behavior. The more you know, the better choices you'll make when you socialize online.

WHY ARE SOCIAL NETWORKING SITES SO POPULAR?

Back in the dark ages of computing, when a mainframe needed a huge room and took hours to print a report, a select few people knew how to program them. They spoke strange languages, like FORTRAN and COBOL. Over time, a man named Tim Berners-Lee decided the common user needed code that was easy to navigate—and more importantly, could find and fix simple display errors. The friendlier HTML was born.

Today, you don't need tech training to inhabit your own corner of the Internet. HTML and WYSIWYG (What You See Is What You Get) editors used by social networking sites make it easy to build your own Web page or blog. The sites provide basic design ready for personalization. You upload photos or artwork and decorate your space with someone else's

Celebrities keep it real, 140 characters at a time, on Twitter. Fans relish the daily minutiae. Actors Ashton Kutcher (@aplusk) and Demi Moore (@mrskutcher) are two of the most-read tweeters.

design. Some sites let you add more pages if you want. You can post videos, join groups, or even start your own fan pages.

The popularity of social networking sites has grown exponentially in the last decade. A Kaiser Family Foundation survey conducted recently found that teens spend on average one hour and twenty-two minutes each day doing social networking activities. Many have more than one account. It isn't unusual for a teen to have a Facebook page, a MySpace page, a YouTube account, and Google Chat account.

Some social networking sites are more popular with certain age groups than others. Studies find teen interest in writing or reading blogs has dropped off in the last few years. And many teens say "meh" to Twitter, even with celebrity tweeters like actors Ashton Kutcher and Demi Moore or singer Lady Gaga.

There You Are!

The Web is a giant playground filled with shops and arcade games, gossip and entertainment, news stories, and debates—all things people like. Social networking sites are your home base. You can hang out with friends as you play online. Some sites have their own games that members can play together. On Facebook, Farmville and Mafia War encourage you to recruit new players so that you can earn points and complete tasks. The more you play and get others to play, the better you do in the game. MyYearbook.com has a blind-date game where you pick at least four other members to play with you.

Social networking sites build databases about their members. Users can seek out friends already on a site or invite others to join just by uploading their e-mail contacts. Many sites prompt you with "You might know this person because your friend does" and a list of mutual acquaintances. In other words, the site does most of your networking legwork for you. And that's how it gets its power. It's easy.

Advertisers like social networking sites for the same reason. It's easy for them to find you.

You see, advertisers love teens. You have buying power, and not just with your own money. Statistics show many teens influence how and where their parents spend billions of dollars each year. Advertisers and marketing whizzes aren't dumb. They hope to forge brand loyalty now that will last as you, and your bank account, grow.

Ever notice how the ads on the sides or top of your social networking page relate to some topic you posted recently?

Advertisers spend money and effort to learn what teens do and where they go online. They use data from surveys and tracking cookies to personalize the ads you see when you visit favorite Web sites, including MTV.com (http://www.mtv.com).

Marketers track what you do using keywords and find an ad they hope will entice you to click. Many social networking and gaming sites are geared toward younger children and teens. The sites are free, which draws even more members. But they are filled with advertisements for movies, clothes, and games.

There are links to other sites selling more products. Some links take you to a survey that asks about the music you like, your favorite fast food places, and what clothes you like to wear. These links and ads track where you go and what you look at, then use data from other users to lead you to even more sites selling products. Some sites even seek out teens who have a strong social network to be trendsetters. They give teens free samples to share with friends and request feedback.

It sounds innocent enough. But it becomes dangerous if the sites lead teens or younger children to inappropriate sites. This can happen easily. Many social networking sites require a minimum age and a valid e-mail account. A young person can easily give a fake birth date. If you do this, the site's advertisers think you're older than you really are. They may advertise content better suited to someone who is more emotionally mature, or even adult content. Sometimes advertisers ask for personal data such as addresses or credit card numbers that could compromise your online security.

So What's It to You?

Since the first media programs were broadcast on radio and later on television, adults have tried to protect children from inappropriate messages. They created rating systems for video games, movies, television programs, even music. Ratings let buyers know if the product contains violence, sexual themes, or foul language. But there is no rating system for advertisements.

You may have heard your parents fret that too many television commercials can manipulate a teen's self-esteem or desire to be popular, admired, or respected. They might think all those sexual undertones and overt references are completely unnecessary. They may worry that the ads that bombard you with cries for more-more-more will warp your priorities and stunt your ability to make smart buying choices. They may feel the same way about online advertisers. Many parents worry that there are less and less places for teens to go where marketing messages can't follow.

In the award-winning novel *Feed*, author M. T. Anderson writes of a world literally wired to the consumer Web. The inhabitants of this world have WiFi chips implanted into their brains shortly after birth. This lets them access the universal feed of digital information. In fact, the few who aren't wired find themselves unable to participate or function fully in the world. The feed slams each person 24/7 with flashy advertisements, news sound bites, and a voice telling them what's new, what's hot, what's now.

Every thought is analyzed based on past buying habits to generate another product suggestion. Characters can't think or even dream without being directed to a must-have product. They never learn the nuances of verbal and nonverbal communication. In this world, the president of the United States can't speak a coherent sentence. The people follow where their feeds lead, oblivious to their dying world.

Humans need other humans. They want to be part of a bigger community, to belong. Social networking gives us a chance to do this virtually. But we need to remain aware, as we click on ads we like or follow links to wherever they lead, that marketers nibble up those cookies we leave behind.

While we play, they build consumer profiles to promote their products and services to us. Ultimately it comes down to how

Your parents likely complain that you spend too much time online. Teens nowadays do meet new friends online. The trick is to know the difference between online socializing and real-life relationships.

much you allow yourself to be manipulated by flashy images that suggest you must look or act a certain way. What do you need to feel fulfilled in your life?

Wired—or Rewired?

Your parents probably nag that you spend too much time watching television and playing video games and trolling YouTube. Could so much social interaction via machine be harmful to your health? Brain scientists debate that very idea.

In the book *iBrain: Surviving the Technological Alteration of the Modern Mind*, authors Gary Small and Gigi Vorgan talk about Digital Natives—people who've never known a world without the Internet, computers, twenty-four-hour news programming, text messaging, or search engines. That's you. They say this exposure from toddlerhood on has stunted Digital Natives' one-on-one people skills.

Do teens forgo hanging out together in real life in favor of the virtual scene? Talk to them and they'll all say no. They still flock to movies—*Twilight*, anyone? They pack football stadiums and basketball courts on Friday nights. Malls are filled with flocks of teens flitting from store to food court to store. They call out to each other in school halls, cruise the strip on Saturday nights, and attend dances and house parties.

You need to function in the digital, immediate-response world we've created. You also need the ability to deeply comprehend all the experiences you'll have in life. You'll need empathy that goes beyond emoticons. You'll need the ability to clearly and concisely speak your thoughts as well as fast fingers to text them.

With anything in life, you need balance. Social networking sites make it easy to find and make connections, but humans still need face time in order to truly remain connected to each other.

three

HOW MUCH SHARING AND SHOWING IS TOO MUCH?

Sometimes people get online and think they're anonymous, invisible even. Part of it is because you can turn yourself into any kind of person you want to be. You make up a login username—not your real name—to protect your privacy. You choose an avatar, or picture to represent you—again, not a real picture because we don't want creepy people to know what you look like.

You've got a clever online ID, like jaded_rebel, that really represents who you are. You've got a rocking anime cartoon of yourself for your avatar. You can say what you want to whomever you want because you're no longer Jordan J. from Belton, Missouri. You're jaded_rebel, and you've got attitude.

For some people, a sense of invisibility turns to a sense of invincibility. They say or do things online they'd never do otherwise.

Think about it. Have you ever been rude online when you'd never act that way in real life? Have you made a suggestive comment, knowing you could never say it in front of another person?

"It's harmless," you say to yourself. "Everybody knows I'm not like that in real life. I'm just having fun."

Who Are You?

You have 642 friends on Facebook. When you log in to your favorite gaming community, other players send pop-up messages, glad to see you. Your buddy lists are so deep, someone is always ready to IM in the middle of the night when you're bored.

Look at how many friends you have. They're all real friends, right? Not really.

The sad truth is many teens measure their value based on how popular they are. And so they find more online friends, adding whoever seeks them out or anyone that other friends have on their lists. The number of friends swells. They feel important and wanted.

And then they start sharing. But too many share too much.

You see it all the time. Teens use their social networking pages to tell everyone exactly where they'll be— "mini-golf with Jae!"—and when. They post "So bored. Text me!" followed by their cell number. They upload photos of themselves pouting, tugging their waistbands a little lower, showing more flesh than they normally would.

And sometimes they post secrets about themselves or others. Everybody does it. That makes it OK, right?

No, it doesn't.

Sure, it's OK to give your number to new friends or make plans with the gang to meet at the combination Pizza Hut and Taco Bell. Before MySpace and Facebook brought social networking to the digital world, people made plans by phone, passed notes in class, or just told each other. But it's much easier to send out a blanket announcement on the Web than it is to call each friend, one at a time, to see if they can do something.

And sometimes, when you're feeling insecure or lonely, you just need to get those bad feelings off your chest. And it feels a lot less lonely when a friend reads it and immediately replies back.

Teens used to share deep stuff only with their best friends. Nowadays, some people figure everyone they meet on any social networking site is a BFF.

It's a strange phenomenon that many if not most people experience when they log on. Your actions immediately become visible to anyone. At the same time, you feel immensely quiet and invisible. There is so much out there, to read, to watch, to play. Nobody's paying that much attention to you.

But you're reaching more people than you realize.

Most of the people you interact with online shouldn't know much about you, if anything at all. Regardless of how much time you spend talking about Team Jacob or playing *World of Warcraft*, you do not know the people you meet online. You don't see who they truly are, how they act toward their grandma

Many teens love massive multiplayer online role-playing games. *World of Warcraft* holds the Guinness World Record among other MMORPGs for having the most subscribers—eleven million-plus each month.

or little brother, or if they're kind to stray cats. You don't know if they're even the actual age and sex they claim to be. And you probably need to think about what you're about to post three more times before you hit enter.

The thing is, someone can easily copy and paste all kinds of information about you. Even the people you think you know might not be who they say they are. They can hit "Forward" and share your most intimate secrets with anybody. They can copy your pictures and post them in public places. They can Photoshop something silly, or worse, something hurtful. They can pretend to be someone else.

Let's put it this way. Do you want some creepy guy who leers at you from a van parked in a dark corner to know your full name, address, cell number, where the party is, what time your parents will be gone, where you go to school, or any other detail of your life? Creepy guys like him are online right now, reading about someone just like you.

That's Private!

You'd think teens would know not to post their addresses, passwords, or bank account and Social Security numbers online. Most do know this. But there are lots of other clues you might drop that make it easy for scammers to find you when you visit sites. Smart scammers know how to manipulate a conversation to get the info they need—like your grandma's maiden name, which credit card companies often use to verify a real account holder. Or your student ID. Or any other password you might use for any other reason.

Networking sites encourage sharing because it helps them build a database. They prompt you to fill out surveys, register for "special features," or offer discounts if you "sign up now!" They use all the information you give—your sex, your age, your geographical location, your likes and dislikes—to create user profiles. They use these databases to tempt advertisers to their sites. They also create a personal profile for you called a cookie. Cookies track your logins and passwords so that you can easily reenter a site. But they also track the other places you go, the links you click.

In 2000, Congress passed the Children's Online Privacy Protection Act (COPPA). It specified what information sites must include in their privacy policies, how they will ensure security for young viewers, and how they will verify parental consent. It also outlined exactly what kind of personal information that Web sites could collect from children under thirteen.

What's important to remember here is that COPPA outlines requirements for sites that cater exclusively to younger children. For the most part, legitimate sites rely on the honesty and common sense of the people who visit. They rely on parents to watch out and protect their children from heading off into sleazy parts of town.

COPPA doesn't prevent older teens who should know better from sometimes blurting out private information. It doesn't protect children who lie about their birth dates to visit inappropriate sites and hide their wayward surfing from parents.

COPPA's guidelines on privacy carry over into social networking sites. A legitimate site makes it easy for users to opt out of sharing personal information with potential advertisers, such as their geographical location, age, or sex.

Protecting Your Identity

When choosing social networking sites, look for security features that let you block unwelcome content or people. You want friend filters so that you can pick and choose who can see certain photos or posts. Instructions on how to make a formal complaint against any user who acts threatening or inappropriate should be easy to find and understand.

When it comes to putting yourself online, the magic words again are "common sense." Social networking sites trust that you'll be smart about sharing your personal life with others. The

Passwords can only protect you so much when you're online. You also need to be smart about privacy settings on your social networking pages.

sites don't protect you from possible harm that comes from sharing otherwise obvious information, like images of your face or your friends' names.

Alexis (not her real name) is a sixteen-year-old sophomore who lives in the Midwest. She, like many teens, started a Facebook account a few year ago. In no time, she had become online friends with several hundred teens. They found each other through mutual friends, on fan pages, comments left on others' walls, and so on.

Alexis posted lots of pictures and set her privacy settings to "friends and friends of friends." The pictures included some of her family, her softball team, and her and her best friend puckering up for the camera. She logged onto Facebook several times a week.

One day in the fall of 2009, Alexis received an IM from a school friend. The friend wanted to know what was going on with the weird posts and links Alexis made on her other Facebook page. At first it was funny, her friend said, but it was getting weird. Alexis acted like two different people on her different accounts.

Alexis's social identity had been stolen. She told her parents right away. They found out that a few weeks earlier dozens of her friends received new invitations to be friends. The request came with a user pic of Alexis. The username had changed, but it was similar enough and still a play on Alexis's name. Her friends figured Alexis had forgotten her password and had to create a second account or maybe just wanted two accounts—one her parents knew about and one they didn't.

Only accepted friends could see the bogus Alexis's details, so the real Alexis couldn't tell who created the account. But the fake user photo was one she'd posted on her account. They had many of the same friends, but the fake Alexis had befriended people the real Alexis didn't know.

Alexis's parents contacted the police, the Kansas Bureau of Investigation, and Facebook. The crime lines were blurry at best. The fake Alexis hadn't threatened anyone. She hadn't tried to use the real Alexis's financial information. She hadn't uploaded pornography or directed anyone to pornographic sites.

Some scammers have been stealing identities longer than you've been on the planet. Don't share information with your social networking site beyond what's required, and don't make the information public.

They had to prove the fake Alexis had malicious intent to harm or defraud.

Alexis's parents and their friends sent friend requests to the fake Alexis, hoping to discover who it was. The requests went ignored. They sent private messages telling the thief to stop posing as Alexis or they would prosecute. The fake Alexis canceled the account shortly after.

Alexis's story didn't have a tragic ending. It didn't make the news. She was lucky she even found out about it.

The real Alexis canceled her Facebook account and started a new, private one. She invites only people she knows personally and locks everything on the tightest privacy setting available. She doesn't accept friend requests from anyone she hasn't met first, even if they have mutual friends. Her online friend list is a lot shorter now, but, she says with confidence, she knows they are friends.

People can manipulate you through the information you share online. And sometimes, that manipulation can put you in an uncomfortable situation.

Myths and Facts

You're only important if you have lots of online friends.

Fact ➡ This is absolutely false on so many levels. Don't base your sense of self-worth on meaningless measurements like whether you look popular online. Your value as a human being doesn't depend on a social graph that exists only in a digital world. If you've connected with a lot of people online, that means only one thing: you've found a lot of people who joined the same social networking site you did.

People love and value you for you, regardless of how many online buddies you collect. Virtual friendships are fleeting. Focus on reality. When it comes to friends, quality, not quantity, will always matter most.

If you aren't viral, you aren't doing it right.

Fact ➡ It would be so amazing to put something online that seven million viewers have seen, teens reenact for a high school talent show, and even your phys ed teacher has viewed. For every "Dramatic Prairie Dog" there are tens, if not hundreds, of thousands of videos that get maybe sixty-eight views. And for every blog or pic that Boing Boing links to, there are hundreds of unseen things that are just as brilliant or funny.

Don't worry about the number of hits or comments you get. When you put something in a public forum, you will get backlash from total strangers. Absolutely do not get involved in a flame war with a forum troll. People who live to spread negativity or vulgarity have nothing better going on in their lives. Pity them and ignore their ugly comments.

If your friends invite you to play online quizzes or games through a social networking site, it's perfectly safe.

Fact ➥ Not necessarily. At the least, these games require you to register with their sites. This lets them collect marketing information from you, such as your geographic location, your age and sex, and your interests. Usually they use the data to lure advertisers to their site. They might even sell information about users, including you, to other sites that will spam you with invitations to join. Much rarer, but also much worse, a quiz might be a phishing scam designed to get you to share passwords, banking information, or more.

Surveys and quizzes can be a ton of fun. Just keep an eye out for warning flags. Exit immediately if the quiz asks you to enter your password or provide a credit card number, or requires you to provide a mailing address and phone number.

four

WHY DO ADULTS THINK HANGING OUT ONLINE IS SO DANGEROUS?

For many people, the clear picture of what's socially acceptable blurs when they're online. Sometimes the line between what's morally or legally right and wrong gets smudged. Add in the oversharing we talked about in chapter 3 and you've got a potential for big trouble.

Some people start with playful flirting or teasing. They find someone who plays along. But one person takes it further. The back-and-forth turns explicit or cruel. Some people do this on purpose. They like to manipulate, taunt, or hurt others.

Bullying, Cyber-Style

You can make friends on social networking sites, but you also can find jerks. Bullies exist wherever humans interact.

Victims used to get breaks once in a while. Bullies weren't in their faces 24/7. The digital revolution changed that. Bullies now have all kinds of tools—cell phones, Web sites, social networking accounts, gaming communities, and instant messaging—to beat their victims down.

Imagine how awful it must feel. Each time you check your cell, e-mail, personal Web page, gaming sites, you wonder, "Is an ugly message going to slap me in the face?" In *Cyberbullying and Cyberthreats*, Nancy Willard labeled common online bullying situations:

Denigration is a form of public humiliation, only the victim doesn't directly receive the hurtful messages. A bully posts untrue or cruel "news" about a person and sends it to others. In other cases, the bully might use a social networking site to slam a victim. The bully locks or filters the post so that the victim doesn't see it. Sometimes the denigration is a photo or a video, passed around by e-mail, texting, or online forums. In one case, bullies built a Web site just to make fun of their victim.

Exclusion occurs when bullies decide one person shouldn't be part of the crowd. The bullies get others to exclude the victim from online activities, gaming, or buddy lists. This social death can isolate and devastate a victim.

Flaming is an argument between two or more people. It usually happens in a public forum but can happen in private. They trade insults, call each other names, or use vulgar language. A flame war happens when those involved won't

Bullies used Web sites and text messages to taunt Ryan Halligan and spread rumors about his sexuality. Ryan was thirteen years old when he committed suicide in 2003.

stop replying to each other. In public sites, flames can take over a discussion thread. Sometimes "bystanders" join in so that the war keeps going. People in gaming communities who like to taunt other players are called griefers.

Harassment happens when one or more people gang up on someone. The bullies send insulting or offensive texts, instant messages, and e-mails. "Everybody hates you, freak." Sometimes bullies recruit people who don't know the victim to join in, such as friends from a social networking site or gaming community. The victim's replies might be just as insulting or angry, but harassment differs from flaming because the victim wants it to end.

Impersonation is similar to the identity theft we talked about in chapter 3. A bully uses the victim's e-mail, cell phone, social networking site, or instant message identity. Sometimes bullies want to learn something personal about the unsuspecting person who gets the message, then spread it around. Sometimes bullies send hurtful, suggestive, or even sexual or threatening messages.

Outing happens when a bully makes a private conversation public. Sometimes the bully might impersonate a friend of the victim's or convince the victim that he or she wants to be friends. Once the victim reveals something personal or embarrassing, the bully forwards the message to others or posts it online.

Trickery is similar to outing. The victim thinks the communication is private, such as instant messaging or texting, but more people are secretly watching on the bully's end. The bully might try to get the victim to share a secret or make a cruel remark about a person listening in. Sometimes trickery happens when two teens are sexting, or sending sexually explicit text messages or photos to each other.

Cyberstalking is online bullying so extreme it scares a victim. The stalker repeatedly sends intimidating or vulgar messages, videos, or photos. There might be threats, either physical or of destroying friendships and reputations. There might be other forms of bullying, too, such as denigration or impersonation. Many victims know their cyberstalkers, often very well. Stalking is a crime in most jurisdictions.

In 2007, two teen girls used a fake identity on MySpace to send hurtful messages to thirteen-year-old Megan Meier. Megan hanged herself. A mother of one of the teens later admitted to helping create the fake account.

Every day someone somewhere comes across an online bully. Often, the bully and victim know each other. It starts with a perceived insult, moves to a sarcastic reply, then at some point turns ugly. Friends get sucked in because of a warped sense of loyalty. Bystanders egg it on. The drama is better than homework!

You've likely come across someone bullying another person online. Maybe you laughed at a couple of posts or even forwarded one to other friends. Maybe you thought some were a little harsh. But nobody gets hurt for real, right?

Google Megan Meier.

And Ryan Halligan.

And Rachael Neblett.

And Jeffrey Johnston.

And Phoebe Prince.

Cyberthreats

Cyberthreats can be sent from bullies to victims, but a person can also threaten to harm himself or herself. Nancy Willard identifies two forms: direct threat and distressing material.

With direct threats, people state outright their intention to hurt someone, even if they're talking about themselves. They might post a specific attack plan at a school or public place, or describe themselves in the middle of the destruction. A teen might talk about how good it feels to cut her skin or describe how he would kill himself.

Distressing materials are hints in posts, videos, pictures, and other online materials. These hints show the person could be harmful or emotionally unstable. Distressing materials can be words—angry outbursts or despondent remarks. Images can be bloody or violent. Some pose with weapons.

We all have bad days. Sometimes you need to vent that frustration. Some teens have a flair for the dramatic. They act out. They go overboard. Then, they get a reaction and feel better. When does venting cross over into threats or distressing messages? Consider these three examples. Willard covers them more extensively in her book:

"...All I want to do is kill and injure as many of you [...] as I can."
Eric Harris of Littleton, Colorado, posted this online. On April 20, 1999, Harris and Dylan Klebold killed thirteen people at Columbine High before killing themselves. They were eighteen and seventeen years old.

"I'm starting to regret sticking around, I should've taken the razor blade express last time around." Jeff Weise of Red Lake, Minnesota, reportedly posted this in his blog. On March 21, 2005, the seventeen-year-old killed nine people, including his grandfather, before killing himself.

"I cant [sic] imagine going through life without killing a few people...yep people can be kissing my shotgun straight out of doom." Andrew Osantowski of Clinton Township, Michigan, shared this in a private chat with a friend. The friend told her father, and they reported it to Clinton Township's police. Investigators found explosives and multiple weapons at the Osantowski home. Andrew allegedly had plans for a "Columbine-style massacre" at the high school where he'd just enrolled ten days before his arrest. He is now in prison.

It's hard for police and parents to gauge whether teens are blowing off steam or making genuine threats. The First Amendment says we can express ourselves publicly without punishment, as long as we don't threaten harm or encourage others to act violently.

The intent to do harm is clear when someone attacks you physically. It's easy to show this if someone threatens you in person or writing. Digitally, things get fuzzy fast. Words can be copied and altered. A public forum is like a crowded stadium. Are we certain the threat was meant for a specific person?

At what point can authorities step in without violating a person's civil rights? These posts disturb us, but we know the aftermath. Would we recognize the words as threats if our best friend or little brother made them in passing? Would we believe they could hurt someone?

Nowadays, many schools and communities err on the side of caution. They have zero-tolerance policies for anyone caught with weapons, drawing graffiti, fighting, or making threats in person or online. Schools monitor online activities of students during the school day.

Recently, parents of a seventeen-year-old student at Harriton High School in Pennsylvania accused school officials of invading their son's privacy. Their son, like other students, had a school-issued laptop to use at home and school. The parents said school officials had used the computer's built-in Web cam to film their son at home. Harriton's assistant principal allegedly told the student he had a photo of the boy using the school-issued laptop to engage in improper activities as outlined in the school policy.

To live together in society, we agree to give up the ability to do whatever we want, whenever we want. We live by rules and laws so that we can live in safety. You break the rules, you face the consequences.

What is fair and still safe? What is morally right? What is reasonable, normal behavior, and how should that make a difference in the way you act online?

Predators

Sometimes teens use social networking to hurt themselves. They find groups who encourage these unsafe actions. Some

Many schools require their students to sign behavior agreements before going online. Teens need to be smart and respectful when using public computers.

groups lure vulnerable teens who think the sites offer adventure or acceptance.

Cutting, bulimia, and anorexia communities provide a warped sense of control for some teens who feel unwanted, unimportant, or stressed to be perfect. Gambling sites give an adrenaline rush that usually leaves players robbed. Hate groups feed aggression and a distorted sense of entitlement. Suicide or drug communities support each other's desires. Fringe groups preach anticonformity or antisocial lifestyles.

These sites often have discussion forums where lonely teens can find what they consider support. Finally, teens think, people who really understand what I'm going through. The problem is they don't always get the guidance they need to cope, grow, leave potentially destructive behaviors behind, and truly accept and love themselves.

Often instead of helping, communities offer lonely teens tips to continue hurting themselves or others. Members share techniques and ways to avoid getting caught. They form pacts. They plot. They feed off each other's vulnerabilities and emotions. They build a wall, however flimsy, of protection and unity. In a sense, they prey on each other's unstable emotions to justify their own instabilities.

And other predators know this.

The inflated sense of worldliness many teens feel leads to a false sense of security, especially when they can hide in their rooms behind their computers. They connect with another teens or maybe younger adults virtually, but it feels more real than real life.

Here is one example of something that could potentially happen: a fourteen-year-old rape victim uses anorexia to feel in control. She finds an online community where other teen girls talk about restricting themselves, or using laxatives the second they think they've gain a pound, or the fastest ways to induce vomiting without parents finding out. The girl opens up about her rape in a sexual abuse thread. A sixteen-year-old gymnast posts how the girl's story has given her courage to admit her uncle once fondled her. In time, one sends the other a direct message. They exchange cell phone numbers. Soon they're texting each other throughout the day. They share more personal information about where they live or go to school, then intimate thoughts. The sixteen-year-old suggests they meet.

Online predators groom their victims. They use flattery, shared experiences, or empathy. Vulnerable teens fall under the spell. The predator builds trust, which turns to emotional dependence. Eventually the predator controls everything.

In the back of your mind, you know any stranger can claim to be whatever he or she wants online. How do you know for sure that a sixteen-year-old gymnast isn't a fifty-year-old registered sex offender? Photos and avatars aren't proof. You don't see your online friends unless you chat via Skype or send videos. Even then, can you be sure the person you trust is truly the person he or she claims to be?

You know it's dangerous to meet an online friend in person without telling your parents or other trusted adult. You've heard the urban legends about the teen who snuck out of her home to meet an online friend alone and was never seen again. You, like thousands of other teens, say, "I'd never be that stupid." Yet somewhere right now, some predator is online, tracking prey.

Staying safe is more than knowing potential dangers. You need adults you can trust to talk to about weird or ugly things you might experience online. You need to recognize manipulation and bullying and take it seriously. You need faith in your instincts to know when lines have been crossed and the courage to refuse to be part of it. You need to be smart and aware of how you use social networking.

Ten Great Questions to Ask Yourself Before You Post or Text

1 Would you shout it in the middle of the mall or your school cafeteria, with your crush, your guidance counselor, and your mom standing three feet away from you?

2 Would you shout it if you noticed some creepy guy leering at you from a van parked nearby in the dark?

3 If the comment is about someone else, would you say it to that person's face?

4 Would you say it in front of the other person's parents or siblings?

5 If someone else said something similar about you, would you want them to shout it in the middle of the mall or school cafeteria, in front of your crush/guidance counselor/mom?

6 If it's a picture or video, would you show it to your grandmother, your next-door neighbor, or your algebra teacher?

7 If the video or picture is of someone else, would you want that person to post a similar image of you?

8 Would you feel OK if someone copied your post, video, or picture and passed it around to others without your consent?

9 Would it be OK with you if creepy van guy saw it on some random site?

10 If you answered no to any of these questions, do you really want to hit "Enter"?

five

HOW CAN I CONVINCE MY PARENTS I'LL BE SMART AND SAFE ONLINE?

Your relationship with your parent or parents is unique. If you're truly lucky, you feel comfortable asking hard questions and trust you'll get a straight answer. Many teens believe they have a less-than-ideal relationship with their parents. "I can't talk to her! All he does is yell! They'd totally ground me forever if they found out!"

An unfortunate number of teens truly are stuck with parents who don't communicate or respect their children. The parents don't establish clear rules and expectations based on love, affection, and trust. In the worst cases, the parents are abusive and neglectful. If this is you, you need other adults in your life for guidance. Talk to a school counselor, a teacher, or another relative.

No teen wants an adult lurking, watching, reading, or commenting on everything that happens. But you need to be smart about how much you share and what you do online. Trust the adults in your life and let them trust you.

Mutual Trust and Respect

Most parents want to trust their teens. They want to feel confident their teens will make smart, moral choices. At the same time, adults know how harsh the world can be and how one moment of carelessness can lead to tragedy. They know you're still learning about life and the world. You're still growing and changing.

So they worry. They try to protect you. That's their job.

How can you convince your parents or guardians that you're the wise, clever, moral person they want you to be? To earn another's trust, each side must be willing to trust as well. If you hide things from your parents, you don't trust them. How can they trust you in return? Try these steps:

1. **Share your passwords for your e-mail, phone, and social networking sites.** Ack! you say. Give up my privacy? Yes. This simple act tells your parents or the adult in your life that you won't do anything online that you wouldn't want them to see or hear. They've already seen you at your silliest, your most emotional, and your temperamental worst. In all honesty, it's hard for the typical teen to truly freak out the typical parent.

   Trust them on this one. They'll widen your space as long as they can still see their boundaries. They might check up on you—let's face it, they probably will check up on you once in a while. If you act like yourself online, you have little to worry about. But what if you're hurting or hiding from yourself online? Your parents or other adults in your life need to know so they can help you.

2. **Occasionally go through your friends lists with them and tell them more about anyone they might not know.** "Shi'anna is in my algebra class. Derron works with me." Reassure them you aren't befriending random, weirdo psychjobs.

   On that note, don't befriend strangers on any site where they can learn personal information about you, like where you live, go to school, and so on. Keep it on the public boards or in the gaming community.

3. **Tell an adult if something happens that upsets or bothers you.** You probably worry your parents will react badly if you mention someone sent you a pornographic link or a threatening message, and rightly so. Most parents will feel upset on the inside, even if they look calm and reassuring on the outside. Remember: their jobs are to worry about and protect you.

This advice goes for anything that happens to you, whether online or in person. If your parents tend to react emotionally when you're upset, wait until you calm down enough to talk clearly. If you can't talk to your parents about it, tell an adult you do know and trust, such as a teacher, a guidance counselor, or the parent of a friend.

But My Parents Really, Really Can't Know

Some teens do get in over their heads online. What if you have a huge gambling debt? What if you visit self-injury discussion boards? What if you bully or stalk someone, post random threats, or upload disturbing images and videos? You need help. Now. Talk to a teacher, a minister, a family member you can trust.

And if you think sexting with friends or strangers is no big deal, think again. First of all, images and words can be copied, uploaded, and shared. Second, it's against the law to send

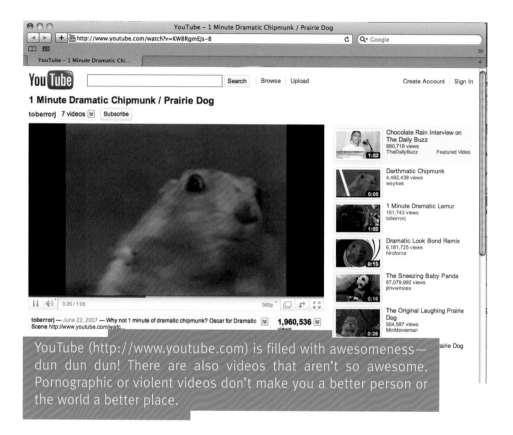

YouTube (http://www.youtube.com) is filled with awesomeness—dun dun dun! There are also videos that aren't so awesome. Pornographic or violent videos don't make you a better person or the world a better place.

pornographic materials of underage teens and children electronically or by mail, even if the images you share are of yourself. Pornography is about control and domination, not mutual love or even just getting off for kicks. That's not how sex should be.

OK, I Get It Now

Reassuring your parents that you can make smart, safe choices online means open communication, mutual respect, and trust. How does that happen?

The Cyber-Safe Kids, Cyber-Savvy Teens Web site offers a teen-parent agreement form. You and your parents or guardian can personalize it to suit your expectations and commitments. The parent agreement says in part that the adult will:

- Pay attention to what you are doing online so that you can discuss issues that might arise together
- Respect your private online communications unless there are significant concerns
- Not overreact should a concern arise
- Fully explain reasons for any restrictions, and offer ways you can regain lost privileges

The teen agreement outlines an action plan you agree to follow to protect your privacy and reputation. You can list sites and activities you will avoid, what you'll do if a stranger approaches you, how you'll handle bullying, and what you'll do if something worries or upsets you. It includes agreements about time limits, any boundaries and restrictions, and how you'll work together to resolve concerns.

It all seems so formal—seriously, I need a contract?—but written agreements let your parents or guardians know you will be responsible for your online actions. You recognize the privilege and the risks of social networking. And really, you just want to have fun. That's what being a teen is all about.

So, make an action plan. Know your assets and risks. Keep your friends close. And have fun storming those social networking castles.

cookie A tracking code used by most Web sites to track where you go online; remembers logins and passwords for specific sites.

COPPA Children's Online Privacy Protection Act; a law that limits the amount of personal data that sites can collect from users under thirteen years old.

cyberthreat Any threat made online or via text.

discussion board A community site where many users can post about shared interests; also called forum.

flaming The exchange of insulting or vulgar messages between two or more people.

forum troll Someone who posts a lot of comments on community message boards.

griefers Bullies on online gaming sites.

grooming What a predator does to build trust or affection from a potential victim.

identity theft When someone pretends to be you or steals your password to certain communities.

lurk To read posts at a community site, social networking site, or discussion board but not interact with anyone.

MMORPG Massively multiplayer online role-playing game, such as *World of Warcraft*.

online predator Someone who builds online friendships with the intent to harm.

opt in/opt out Your choice to let social networking sites or other Web sites share your personal or financial information with third-party users, such as advertisers.

peer-to-peer software Also called P2P or file-sharing; this lets two computers share files or other information without having to go through a central, shared computer.

phishing An online scam that appears to be a legitimate business. The goal is to get personal information, such as passwords or access to financial files.

privacy settings Your control over who can contact you or see what you've uploaded onto a social networking site. This is different from a privacy policy, which companies must post so you know how they share the information they gather about you with third-party users.

sexting Sending explicit, sexual messages, photos, or videos to another person.

social graph A map of all your relationships in your social networks.

stalker Someone who won't leave another person alone. This can be physical contact, but often the stalker lurks out of site.

vlog A specialized blog post that points to a streaming media file instead of a Web page.

Common Sense Media
650 Townsend Street, Suite 375
San Francisco, CA 94103
(415) 863-0600
Web site: http://www.commonsensemedia.org
Common Sense Media is a nonprofit, nonpartisan organization. It provides tools and information to help parents
make informed choices about the media kids use.

Federal Trade Commission (FTC)
Consumer Response Center
600 Pennsylvania Avenue NW
Washington, DC 20580
(877) 382-4357 (FTC HELP)
Web sites: http://www.ftc.gov
http://www.OnGuardOnline.gov
The FTC helps prevent fraudulent, deceptive, and unfair
business practices and helps consumers learn how to spot
and stop them. OnGuardOnline.gov offers tips and games
to help Internet users protect themselves from fraud.

Media Awareness Network
1500 Merivale Road, 3rd floor
Ottawa, ON K2E 6Z5

Canada
(613) 224-7721
Web site: http://www.media-awareness.ca
   Media Awareness Network is a nonprofit group to help
   adults teach their children how media can affect their
   lifestyles and choices. It offers interactive games for children of different ages on its Web site.

National Center for Missing and Exploited Children
Charles B. Wang International Children's Building
699 Prince Street
Alexandria, VA 22314-3175
(800) THE-LOST (843-5678)
Web sites: http://www.missingkids.com
http://www.netsmartz.org
The NCMEC is a private, nonprofit organization that works
   to prevent child abduction and sexual exploitation and to
   find missing children. The group helps victims of child
   abduction and sexual exploitation, their families, and the
   professionals who serve them.

National Cyber Security Alliance
1010 Vermont Avenue NW, Suite 821
Washington, DC 20005
Web site: http://www.staysafeonline.org
The NCSA is a nonprofit partnership of the Department of
   Homeland Security, the Federal Trade Commission, and
   private groups.

Public Safety Canada
269 Laurier Avenue West
Ottawa, ON K1A 0P8
Canada
(800) 830-3118
Web site: http://www.safecanada.ca
Public Safety Canada is a comprehensive government service
    to help citizens stay safe and feel secure. It offers Internet
    safety tips on cyberbullying, spyware, and more.

SocialSafety.org
280 Union Square Drive
New Hope, PA 18938
Web site: http://www.socialsafety.org
Social Safety helps teach teens about social networking's
    potential dangers. The program was built by MyYearbook's
    teen founders Dave and Catherine Cook.

Web Sites

Due to the changing nature of Internet links, Rosen Publishing
has developed an online list of Web sites related to the subject
of this book. This site is updated regularly. Please use this link
to access the list:

http://www.rosenlinks.com/faq/soci

For Further Reading

Anderson, M.T. *Feed*. New York, NY: HarperCollins, 2005.

Bailey, Diane. *Cyber Ethics*. New York, NY: Rosen Publishing Group, 2008.

Boger, Ann. *Frequently Asked Questions About Online Romance*. New York, NY: Rosen Publishing Group, 2007.

Farmer, Leslie. *Teen Girls and Technology: What's the Problem, What's the Solution?* New York, NY: Teachers College Press, 2008.

Farnham, Kevin, and Dale Farnham. *MySpace Safety: 51 Tips for Teens and Parents*. Pomfret: CT. How-To Primers, 2006.

Finn, Katie. *Top 8*. New York, NY: Point, 2009.

Fodeman, Doug, and Marje Monroe. *Safe Practices for Life Online: A Guide for Middle and High School*. Washington, DC: International Society for Technology in Education, 2009.

Gosney, John W. *Blogging for Teens*. Boston, MA: Thomson Course Technology PTR, 2004.

Green, John. *An Abundance of Katherines*. New York, NY: Penguin, 2006.

Green, John. *Paper Towns*. New York, NY: Penguin, 2009.

Hinduja, Sameer, and Justin W. Patchin. *Bullying Beyond the Schoolyard: Preventing and Responding to Cyberbullying*. Thousand Oaks, CA: Corwin Press, 2008.

Kelsey, Candice. *Generation MySpace: Helping Your Teen Survive Online Adolescence.* New York, NY: Marlowe & Co., 2007.

McCarthy, Linda. *Own Your Own Space: Keep Yourself and Your Stuff Safe Online.* Upper Saddle River, NJ. Addison-Wesley, 2006.

Rogers, Vanessa. *Cyberbullying: Activities to Help Children and Teens to Stay Safe in a Texting, Twittering, Social Networking World.* London, England: Jessica Kingsley Publishers, 2010.

Strasser, Todd. *Wish You Were Dead.* New York, NY: Egmont, 2009.

Allen, Richard. "Working Together for Online Safety."
    Facebook, December 6, 2009. Retrieved December 7, 2009
    (http://blog.facebook.com/blog.php?post=195195332130).

CNN.com. "FBI Investigates Allegations Webcam Used to
    Monitor Student." February 22, 2010. Retrieved March 7,
    2010 (http://www.cnn.com/2010/CRIME/02/20/
    laptop.suit/index.html).

Common Sense Media. "Internet Safety Scorecard."
    June 2008. Retrieved March 5, 2010 (http://www.
    commonsensemedia.org/sites/default/files/Internet%20
    Safety%20Scorecard%202008.pdf).

Coursey, David. "Facebook Privacy Changes Go Live;
    Beware of 'Everyone.'" *PC World*, December 9, 2009.
    Retrieved January 7, 2010 (http://www.pcworld.com/
    businesscenter/article/184090/facebook_privacy_
    changes_go_live_beware_of_everyone.html).

Federal Trade Commission. "Social Networking Sites:
    Safety Tips for Tweens and Teens." May 2006. Retrieved
    December 18, 2009 (http://www.ftc.gov/bcp/edu/pubs/
    consumer/tech/tec14.shtm).

Hachman, Mark. "Blogs Just Aren't Cool Any More,
    Teens Say." *PC Magazine*, February 3, 2010. Retrieved
    February 17, 2010 (http://www.pcmag.com/article2/
    0,2817,2358789,00.asp).

Hempel, Jessi, with Paula Lehman. "The MySpace Generation." *Business Week*, December 12, 2005. Retrieved January 7, 2010 (http://www.businessweek.com/magazine/content/05_50/b3963001.htm).

Lenhart, Amanda. "Pew Internet Project Data Memo, Re: Adults and Social Network Websites." Pew Internet & American Life Project, January 14, 2009. Retrieved December 14, 2009 (http://www.pewinternet.org/~/media//Files/Reports/2009/PIP_Adult_social_networking_data_memo_FINAL.pdf.pdf).

Lenhart, Amanda, and Mary Madden. "Pew Internet Project Data Memo, Re: Social Network Sites and Teens: An Overview." Pew Internet & American Life Project, January 3, 2007. Retrieved December 14, 2009 (http://www.pewinternet.org/Reports/2007/Social-Networking-Websites-and-Teens.aspx).

Magid, Leroy, and Anne Collier. *MySpace Unraveled: A Parent's Guide to Teen Social Networking*. Berkeley, CA. Peachpit Press, 2007.

Make a Difference for Kids. "Rachael's Story." Retrieved March 5, 2010 (http://www.makeadifferenceforkids.org/rachael.html).

McCabe, Kathy. "Teen's Suicide Prompts a Look at Bullying." *Boston Globe*, January 24, 2010. Retrieved March 5, 2010 (http://www.boston.com/news/education/k_12/articles/2010/01/24/teens_suicide_prompts_a_look_at_bullying).

The Neilsen Company. "How Teens Use Media." June 2009. Retrieved December 18, 2009 (http://en-us.nielsen.com/etc/medialib/nielsen_dotcom/en_us/documents/pdf/white_papers_and_reports.Par.48571.File.dat/Nielsen_HowTeensUseMedia_June2009.pdf).

Small, Gary, and Gigi Vorgan. *iBrain: Surviving the Technological Alteration of the Modern Mind*. New York, NY: HarperCollins, 2008.

Tiegerman, Dr. Ellenmorris. "Why Are Children with Disabilities Bullied?" LongIslandPress.com, February 22, 2010. Retrieved March 5, 2010 (http://www.longislandpress.com/2010/02/22/why-are-children-with-disabilities-bullied).

Willard, Nancy E. *Cyberbullying and Cyberthreats: Responding to the Challenge of Online Social Aggression, Threats, and Distress*. Champaign, IL: Research Press, 2007.

Willard, Nancy E. *Cyber-Safe Kids, Cyber-Savvy Teens: Helping Young People Learn to Use the Internet Safely and Responsibly*. Hoboken, NJ: Wiley, 2007.

Young Adult Library Services Association. "Teens & Social Networking in School & Public Libraries: A Toolkit for Librarians & Library Workers." Retrieved January 15, 2010 (http://www.ila.org/netsafe/SocialNetworkingToolkit.pdf).

About the Author

When Colleen Ryckert Cook isn't writing fiction and nonfiction for children and teens, she writes about business and management for adults and spends more time than necessary on Facebook and Twitter.

Photo Credits

Cover Jack Hollingsworth/Photodisc/Thinkstock; p. 5 Michael Caulfield/WireImage/Getty Images; p. 7 Bloomberg via Getty Images; p. 10 AFP/Getty Images; pp. 14, 36, 38 © AP Images; p. 19 Liquidlibrary/Thinkstock; pp. 24–25 Nigel Treblin/AFP/ Getty Images; p. 28 Laurence Dutton/The Image Bank/Getty Images; p. 30 Phil Velasquez/MCT/Landov; p. 42 krtphotos/ Newscom; p. 47 Dylan Ellis/Stone/Getty Images.

Designer: Evelyn Horovicz; Editor: Bethany Bryan; Photo Researcher: Peter Tomlinson